Knit

MW00901697

The Ultimate Patterns Book About Knitting Shawls

Copyright © 2023

DEDICATION

Contents

I. Heirloom Knit Shawl

MATERIALS

Patons® Kroy Socks™ (1.75 oz/50 g; 166 yds/152 m)

Flax (55011) 8 balls

Size U.S. 5 (3.75 mm) knitting needles.

U.S. 5 (3.75 mm) circular knitting needle 36" [90 cm] long or size needed to obtain gauge.

ABBREVIATIONS

Alt = Alternate(ing)

Inc = Increasing

K = Knit

K1B = knit into back of next st

K2tog = Knit next 2 stitches together

Kfb = Increase 1 stitch by knitting into front and back of next stitch

P = Purl

P1B = purl into back of next st

PM = Place marker

Psso = Pass slipped stitch over

RS = Right side

Sl1 = Slip next stitch knitwise

St(s) = Stitch(es)

Ssk = Slip next 2 stitches knitwise one at a time. Pass them back onto left-hand needle, then knit through back loops together

WS = Wrong side

Yo = Yarn over

MEASUREMENTS

66" [167.5] wide x 36" [91.5 cm] deep.

GAUGE

26 sts and 34 rows = 4" [10 cm] in stocking st.

INSTRUCTIONS

Note: Work (yo) twice on WS rows as follows:

P1. P1B. With pair of needles, cast on 9 sts. Proceed as follows, noting that work will be moved onto circular needle when pair of needles is no longer sufficient to accommodate sts:

Version I (Work from written instructions only).

Panel I

1st row: (RS). K1B. P2. K1B. (K1. yo. K1) all in next st. K1B. P2. K1B. 11 sts.

2nd and alt rows: Purl. (PM on center st).

3rd row: K1B. P2. K1B. [(K1. yo. K1) in next st] 3 times. K1B. P2. K1B. 17 sts.

5th row: K1B. P2. K1B. Kfb. [(K1. yo. K1) in next st] 7 times. Kfb. K1B. P2. K1B.

7th row: K1B. P2. [K1B. yo. K4. K2tog. (yo) twice. ssk. K4. yo] twice. K1B. P2. K1B.

9th row: K1B. P2. *K1B. yo. K3. [K2tog. (yo) twice. ssk] twice. K3. yo. Rep from * once more. K1B. P2. K1B.

11th row: K1B. P2. *K1B. yo. K2. [K2tog. (yo) twice. ssk] 3 times. K2. yo. Rep from * once more. K1B. P2. K1B.

13th row: K1B. P2. *K1B. yo. K1. [K2tog. (yo) twice. ssk] 4 times. K1. yo. Rep from * once more. K1B. P2. K1B.

15th row: K1B. P2. *K1B. K4. [K2tog. (yo) twice. ssk] 3 times. K4. Rep from * once more. K1B. P2. K1B.

17th row: K1B. P2. *K1B. K2. [K2tog. (yo) twice. ssk] 4 times. K2. Rep from * once more. K1B. P2. K1B.

19th row: K1B. P2. *K1B. (yo. ssk) twice. [K2tog. (yo) twice. ssk] 3 times. (K2tog. yo) twice. Rep from * once more. K1B. P2. K1B.

21st row: K1B. P2. *(K1B. yo) twice. Sl1. K2tog. psso. (yo. ssk. K2tog. yo) 3 times. Sl1. K2tog. psso. yo. K1B. yo. Rep from * once more. K1B. P2. K1B.

23rd row: K1B. P2. *(K1B. yo) 4 times. Sl1. K2tog. psso. (yo. ssk. K2tog. yo) twice. Sl1. K2tog. psso. (yo. K1B) 3 times. yo. Rep from * once more. K1B. P2. K1B.

25th row: K1B. P2. *K1B. yo. (K1B. yo. K2. yo) twice. K1B. yo. Sl1. K2tog. psso. yo. ssk. K2tog. yo. Sl1. K2tog. psso. (yo. K1B. yo. K2) twice. yo. K1B. yo. Rep from * once more. K1B. P2. K1B.

27th row: K1B. P2. K1B. K1. *yo. K1B. yo. K1. ssk. K1. yo. K1B. yo. K1. K2tog. K1. yo. K1B. yo. K1.* Sl1. K2tog. psso. (yo) twice. Sl1. K2tog. psso. K1. Rep from * to* once more. K2tog. Rep from * to * once more. Sl1. K2tog. psso. (yo) twice. Sl1. K2tog. psso. K1. Rep from * to * once more. K1B. P2. K1B.

29th row: K1B. P2. K1B. *K2. yo. K1B. yo. K2. ssk. K1. yo. K1B. yo. K1. K2tog. K2. yo. K1B. yo. (ssk. K2tog) twice. yo. K1B. yo. K2. ssk. K1. yo. K1B. yo. K1. K2tog. K2. yo. K1B. yo. K2. PM for center of Shawl. Rep from * once more. K1B. P2. K1B.

31st row: K1B. P2. K1B. (ssk. K1. yo. K1B. yo. K1. K2tog) 12 times. K1B. P2. K1B.

33rd, 35th and 37th rows: As 31st row.

39th row: K1B. P2. K1B. *yo. ssk. K3. K2tog. yo. ssk. K1. yo. K1B. yo. K1. K2tog. yo. (ssk. K3. K2tog) twice. yo. ssk. K1. yo. K1B. yo. K1. K2tog. yo. ssk. K3. K2tog. Rep from * once more. yo. K1B. P2. K1B.

41st row: K1B. P2. K1B. *yo. K1. yo. ssk. K1. K2tog. yo. K1. yo. ssk. K1. yo. K1B. yo. K1. K2tog. yo. K1. yo. (Ssk. K1. K2tog) twice. yo. K1. yo. ssk. K1. yo. K1B. yo. K1. K2tog. yo. K1. yo. ssk. K1. K2tog. Rep from * once more. yo. K1. yo. K1B. P2. K1B.

43rd row: K1B. P2. K1B. *yo. K3. yo. Sl1. K2tog. psso. yo. K1. ssk. yo. ssk. K1. yo. K1B. yo. K1. K2tog. yo. K2tog. K1. yo. (Sl1. K2tog. psso) twice. yo. K1. ssk. yo. ssk. K1. yo. K1B. yo. K1. K2tog. yo. K2tog. K1. yo. Sl1. K2tog. psso. Rep from * once more. yo. K3. yo. K1B. P2. K1B.

45th row: K1B. P2. K1B. yo. [K2tog. (yo) twice. ssk] twice. K2tog. yo. *Ssk. K1. yo. K1B. yo. K1. K2tog. yo. ssk. K1. (yo) twice. ssk. K2tog. (yo) twice. K1. K2tog. yo. ssk. K1. yo. K1B. yo. K1. K2tog.* yo. K1. K2tog. (yo) twice. ssk. K2tog. (yo) twice. Sl1. K2tog. psso. K2tog. (yo) twice. ssk. K1. yo. Rep from * to * once more. yo. ssk. [K2tog. (yo) twice. ssk] twice. yo. K1B. P2. K1B.

47th row: K1B. P2. K1B. yo. K1. (yo. ssk. K2tog. yo) twice. K2. *yo. ssk. K1. yo. K1B. yo. K1. (K2tog. yo) twice. (yo. ssk. K2tog. yo) twice. (yo. ssk.) twice. K1. yo. K1B. yo. K1. K2tog. yo. K2.* [Ssk. K2tog. (yo) twice] twice. ssk. K2tog. K2. Rep from * to * once more. (yo. ssk. K2tog. yo) twice. K1. yo. K1B. P2. K1B.

49th row: K1B. P2. K1B. yo. K2. *[K2tog. (yo) twice. ssk] twice. K3. yo. ssk. K3. K2tog. yo.* K3. Rep from * to * once more. K2. [K2tog. (yo) twice. ssk] 3 times. K2. yo. ssk. K3. K2tog. yo. K3. Rep from * to * once more. K3. [K2tog. (yo) twice. ssk] twice. K2. yo. K1B. P2. K1B.

51st row: K1B. P2. K1B. yo. K1. *[K2tog. (yo) twice. ssk] 3 times. K2. yo. ssk. K1. K2tog. yo.* K2. Rep from * to * once more. K1. [K2tog. (yo) twice. ssk] 4 times. K1. yo. ssk. K1. K2tog. yo. K2. Rep from * to * once more. K2. [K2tog. (yo) twice. ssk] 3 times. K1. yo. K1B. P2. K1B.

53rd row: K1B. P2. K1B. yo. *[K2tog. (yo) twice. ssk] 4 times. K1. yo. Sl1. K2tog. psso. yo.* K1. Rep from * to * once more. [K2tog. (yo) twice. ssk] 5 times. yo. Sl1. K2tog. psso. yo. K1. Rep from * to * once more. K1. [K2tog. (yo) twice. ssk] 4 times. yo. K1B. P2. K1B.

55th row: K1B. P2. K1B. K1. (yo) twice. ssk. K2tog. (yo) twice. ssk. K4. [K2tog. (yo) twice. ssk] twice. Sl1. K2tog. psso. (yo) twice. ssk. K2tog. (yo) twice. ssk. K4. [K2tog. (yo) twice. ssk] 4 times. K2tog. K4. [Ssk. K2tog. (yo) twice] 4 times. ssk. K4. K2tog. (yo) twice. ssk. K2tog. (yo) twice. Sl1. K2tog. psso. [K2tog (yo) twice. ssk] twice. K4. K2tog. (yo) twice. ssk. K2tog. (yo) twice. K1. K1B. P2. K1B.

56th row: Purl. 55 sts at each side of marker.

Panel II

Work Panel II as follows:

Knit Shawl

1st row: (RS). K1B. P2. K1B. yo. ssk. K2tog. (yo) twice. ssk. K2. K2tog. *(yo) twice. ssk. K2.** [K2tog. (yo) twice. ssk] 3 times. K2. K2tog.* Rep from * to * 3 times more, then from * to ** once K2tog. (yo) twice. ssk. K2tog. yo. K1B. P2. K1B. 108 sts.

2nd and alt rows: Purl.

3rd row: K1B. P2. K1B. K2tog. (yo) twice. ssk. K2tog. yo. K1. K2tog. *yo. K2. yo. ssk. K1.** (yo. ssk. K2tog. yo) 3 times. K1. K2tog. Rep from * 3 times more, then from * to ** once. yo. ssk. K2tog. (yo) twice. ssk. K1B. P2. K1B.

5th row: K1B. P2. K1B. yo. ssk. K2tog. yo. K2. K2tog. *yo. K4. yo. ssk. K2.** (yo. ssk. K2tog. yo) twice. K2. K2tog. Rep from * 3 times more, then from * to ** once. yo. ssk. K2tog. yo. K1B. P2. K1B.

7th row: K1B. P2. K1B. K2tog. (yo) twice. ssk. K1. K2tog. *yo. K1. yo. K4. yo. K1. yo. ssk. K1.** [K2tog. (yo) twice. ssk] twice. K1. K2tog. Rep from * 3 times more, then from * to ** once. K2tog. (yo) twice. ssk. K1B. P2. K1B.

9th row: K1B. P2. K1B. yo. ssk. K2. *(K2tog. yo. K3. yo. ssk) twice. K2. K2tog.** (yo) twice. ssk. K2. Rep from * 3 times more, then from * to ** once. yo. K1B. P2. K1B.

8

11th row: K1B. P2. K1B. *(K2tog. yo. K1) twice. K4. yo. ssk. yo. K4. (K1. yo. ssk) twice. Rep from * 4 times more. K1B. P2. K1B.

13th row: K1B. P2. K1B. *K2. K2tog. yo. K1. yo. ssk. K1. K2tog. yo. K3. yo. ssk. K1. K2tog. yo. K1. yo. ssk. K2. Rep from * 4 times more. K1B. P2. K1B.

15th row: K1B. P2. K1B. *Sl1. K2tog. psso. yo. K3. yo. Sl1. K2tog. psso. yo. K5. yo. Sl1. K2tog. psso. yo. K3. yo. Sl1. K2tog. psso. Rep from * 4 times more. K1B. P2. K1B.

17th row: K1B. P2. K1B. yo. K1. yo. *K5. yo. K9. yo. K5. yo.** K2tog. yo. Rep from * 3 times more, then from * to ** once. K1. yo. K1B. P2. K1B.

19th row: K1B. P2. K1B. yo. *K3. yo. ssk. K1. K2tog. yo. K11. yo. ssk. K1. K2tog. yo. Rep from * 4 times more. K3. yo. K1B. P2. K1B.

21st row: K1B. P2. K1B. yo. *K5. yo. Sl1. K2tog. psso. yo. K5. K2tog. yo. K6. yo. Sl1. K2tog. psso. yo. Rep from * 4 times more. K5. yo. K1B. P2. K1B.

22nd row: Purl.

Panel III

Work Panel III as follows:

1st row: (RS). K1B. P2. K1B. Kfb. yo. ssk. *K1. K2tog. yo. K7. K2tog. yo. K1B. yo. ssk. K7. yo. ssk. Rep from * 4 times more. K1. K2tog. yo. Kfb. K1B. P2. K1B.

2nd and alt rows: Purl.

3rd row: K1B. P2. K1B. yo. K3. *yo. Sl1. K2tog. psso. yo. K6. Sl1. K2tog. psso. yo. K1. yo. K1B. yo. K1. yo. Sl1. K2tog. psso. K6. Rep from * 4 times more. yo. Sl1. K2tog. psso. yo. K3. yo. K1B. P2. K1B.

5th row: K1B. P2. K1B. yo. K1. yo. K9. *K1. Sl1. K2tog. psso. yo. K3. yo. K1B. yo. K3. yo. Sl1. K2tog. psso. K10. Rep from * 4 times more. yo. K1. yo. K1B. P2. K1B.

7th row: K1B. P2. K1B. yo. K3. yo. K1. *K7. Sl1. K2tog. psso. yo. K2tog. yo. K1B. yo. ssk. yo. K1B. yo. K2tog. yo. K1B. yo. ssk. yo. Sl1. K2tog. psso. Rep from * 4 times more. K8. yo. K3. yo. K1B. P2. K1B.

9th row: K1B. P2. K1B. yo. K2. yo. K1B. yo. K2. yo. ssk. K1. *K3. Sl1. K2tog. psso. yo. K2tog. K1. yo. K1B. yo.** K1. ssk. yo. K1B. yo. K2tog. K1. yo. K1B. yo. K1. ssk. yo. Sl1. K2tog. psso.* Rep from * to * once more, then from * to ** once. K3. yo. K1B (center of Shawl). yo. K3. yo. KB1. yo. K1. ssk. yo. Sl1. K2tog. psso. Rep from

10

* to * twice more. K4. K2tog. yo. K2. yo. K1B. yo. K2. yo. K1B. P2. K1B.

11th row: K1B. P2. K1B. yo. K4. yo. K1B. yo. K2. ssk. yo. ssk. K1. Sl1. K2tog. psso. *yo. K2tog. K2.** yo. K1B. yo. K2. ssk. yo. K1B. yo. K2tog. K2. yo. K1B. yo. K2. ssk. yo. ssk. K1. K2tog. Rep from * once more, then from * to ** once. (yo. K1B. yo. K4) twice. *** yo. K1B. yo. K2. ssk. yo.**** Ssk. K1. K2tog. yo. K2tog. K2. yo. K1B. yo. K2. ssk. yo. K1B. yo. K2tog. K2. Rep from *** once more, then from *** to **** once. Sl1. K2tog. psso. K1. K2tog. yo. K2tog. K2. yo. K1B. yo. K4. yo. K1B. P2. K1B.

13th row: K1B. P2. K1B. yo. K1B. *yo. K2tog. K3. yo. K1B. yo. K3. ssk. yo. Sl1. K2tog. psso. yo. K2tog. K3. yo. K1B. yo. K3. ssk. yo. K1B.* Rep from * to * twice more. (yo. K1B) twice. Rep from * to * 3 times more. yo. K1B. P2. K1B. 14th row: Purl.

Panel IV

Work panel IV as follows:

1st row: (RS). K1B. P2. (K1B. yo) twice. *(K1B. yo) twice. ssk. K8. Sl1. K2tog. psso. (yo) twice. ssk. K8. K2tog. yo. K1B. yo.* Rep from * to * twice more. (K1B. yo) 4 times. **(K1B. yo) twice. ssk. K8.

K2tog. (yo) twice. Sl1. K2tog. psso. K8. K2tog. yo. K1B. yo.** Rep from ** to ** twice more. (K1B. yo) twice. K1B. P2. K1B.

2nd and alt rows: Purl.

3rd row: K1B. P2. K1B. K3. yo. *K1B. yo. K3. yo. ssk. K5. Sl1. K2tog. psso. yo. K2. yo. Sl1. K2tog. psso. K5. K2tog. yo. K3. yo.* Rep from * to * twice more. K1B. yo. K3. K1B. K3. yo. Rep from * to * 3 times. K1B. yo. K3. K1B. P2. K1B.

5th row: K1B. P2. K1B. [K1. yo. K1B. yo. ssk. yo. *K1B. yo. K2tog. yo. K1B. (yo. ssk) twice. K3. K2tog. yo. ssk. K2tog. yo. ssk. K3. (K2tog. yo) twice. K1B. yo. ssk. yo. Rep from * twice more. K1B. yo. K2tog. yo. K1B. yo. K1. K1B] twice. P2. K1B.

7th row: K1B. P2. K1B. [K2. yo. K1B. yo. K1. ssk. yo. *K1B. yo. K2tog. K1. yo. K1B. yo. K1. ssk. yo. ssk. K1. K2tog. yo. ssk. K2tog. yo. ssk. K1. K2tog. yo. K2tog. K1. yo. K1B. yo. K1. ssk. yo. Rep from * twice more. K1B. yo. K2tog. K1. yo. K1B. yo. K2. K1B] twice. P2. K1B.

9th row: K1B. P2. K1B. [K3. yo. K1B. yo. K2. ssk. yo. *K1B. yo. K2tog. K2. yo. K1B. yo. K2. ssk. yo. Sl1. K2tog. psso. yo. ssk. K2tog. yo. Sl1. K2tog. psso. yo. K2tog. K2. yo. K1B. yo. K2. ssk. yo. Rep from * twice more. K1B. yo. K2tog. K2. yo. K1B. yo. K3. K1B] twice. P2. K1B.

11th row: K1B. P2. K1B. [K4. yo. K1B. yo. K3. ssk. yo. *K1B. yo. K2tog. K3. yo. K1B. yo. K3. ssk. yo. (Sl1. K2tog. psso) twice. yo. K2tog. K3. yo. K1B. yo. K3. ssk. yo. Rep from * twice more. K1B. yo. K2tog. K3. yo. K1B. yo. K4. K1B] twice. P2. K1B.

12th row: Purl.

Panel V

Work panel V as follows:

1st row: (RS). K1B. P2. K1B. [yo. ssk. K7. K2tog. yo. K1. yo. *K1B. yo. K1. yo. ssk. K8. Sl1. K2tog. psso. (yo) twice. Sl1. K2tog. psso. K8. K2tog. yo. K1. yo. Rep from * twice more. K1B. yo. K1. yo. ssk. K7. K2tog. yo. K1B] twice. P2. K1B.

2nd and alt rows: Purl.

3rd row: K1B. P2. K1B. [yo. K1. yo. ssk. K5. K2tog. yo. K3. yo. *K1B. yo. K3. yo. ssk. K5. Sl1. K2tog. psso. yo. K2. yo. Sl1. K2tog. psso. K5. K2tog. yo. K3. yo. Rep from * twice more. K1B. yo. K3. yo. ssk. K5. K2tog. yo. K1. yo. K1B] twice. P2. K1B.

5th row: K1B. P2. K1B. [yo. K1. K2tog. yo. ssk. K3. (K2tog. yo) twice. K1B. yo. ssk. yo. *K1B. yo. K2tog. yo. K1B. yo. ssk. yo. ssk.

K3. K2tog. yo. ssk.** K2tog. yo. ssk. K3. K2tog. yo. K2tog. yo. K1B. yo. ssk. yo. Rep from * twice more, then from * to ** once more. K1. yo. K1B] twice. P2. K1B.

7th row: K1B. P2. K1B. [yo. K1. Sl1. K2tog. psso. yo. ssk. K1. K2tog. yo. K2tog. K1. yo. K1B. yo. K1. ssk. yo. *K1B. yo. K2tog. K1. yo. K1B. yo. K1. ssk. yo. ssk. K1. K2tog. yo.** Ssk. K2tog. yo. ssk. K1. K2tog. yo. K2tog. K1. yo. K1B. yo. K1. ssk. yo. Rep from * twice more, then from * to ** once more. Sl1. K2tog. psso. K1. yo. K1B] twice. P2. K1B.

9th row: K1B. P2. K1B. [yo. K1. Sl1. K2tog. psso. yo. Sl1. K2tog. psso. yo. K2tog. K2. yo. K1B. yo. K2. ssk. yo. *K1B. yo. K2tog. K2. yo. K1B. yo. K2. ssk. yo. Sl1. K2tog. psso. yo.** Ssk. K2tog. yo. Sl1. K2tog. psso. yo. K2tog. K2. yo. K1B. yo. K2. ssk. yo. Rep from * twice more, then from * to ** once more Sl1. K2tog. psso. K1. yo. K1B] twice. P2. K1B.

11th row: K1B. P2. K1B. [yo. K2. Sl1. K2tog. psso. yo. K2tog. K3. yo. K1B. yo. K3. ssk. yo. *K1B. yo. K2tog. K3. yo. K1B. yo. K3. ssk. yo.** (Sl1. K2tog. psso) twice. yo. K2tog. K3. yo. K1B. yo. K3. ssk. yo. Rep from * twice more, then from * to ** once more. Sl1. K2tog. psso. K2. yo. K1B] twice. P2. K1B.

14

13th row: K1B. P2. K1B. [yo. K1. yo. (Sl1. K2tog. psso) twice. K7. K2tog. yo. K1. yo. *K1B. yo. K1. yo. ssk.** K8. Sl1. K2tog. psso. (yo) twice. Sl1. K2tog. psso. K8. K2tog. yo. K1. yo. Rep from * twice more, then from * to ** once more. K7. (Sl1. K2tog. psso) twice. yo. K1. yo. K1B] twice. P2. K1B.

15th row: K1B. P2. K1B. [yo. K1. yo. K1B. yo. K2. (yo) twice. ssk. K5. K2tog. yo. K3. yo. *K1B. yo. K3. yo. ssk. K5.** Sl1. K2tog. psso yo. K2. yo. Sl1. K2tog. psso. K5. K2tog. yo. K3. yo. Rep from * twice more, then from * to ** once more. K2tog. (yo) twice. K2. yo. K1B. yo. K1. yo. K1B] twice. P2. K1B.

17th row: K1B. P2. K1B. [yo. K2tog. K1. yo. K1B. yo. K1. ssk. yo. K2. yo. ssk. K3. K2tog. yo. K2tog. yo. K1B. yo. ssk. yo. *K1B. yo. K2tog. yo. K1B. yo. ssk. yo. ssk. K3. K2tog. yo.** Ssk. K2tog. yo. ssk. K3. (K2tog. yo) twice. K1B. yo. ssk. yo. Rep from * twice more, then from * to ** once more. K2. yo. K2tog. K1. yo. K1B. yo. K1. ssk. yo. K1B] twice. P2. K1B.

19th row: K1B. P2. K1B. [yo. K2tog. K2. yo. K1B. yo. K3. yo. ssk. K2tog. yo. ssk. K1. K2tog. yo. K2tog. K1. yo. K1B. yo. K1. ssk. yo. *K1B. yo. K2tog. K1. yo. K1B. yo. K1. ssk. yo. ssk. K1. K2tog. yo. ssk. K2tog. yo.** Ssk. K1. K2tog. yo. K2tog. K1. yo. K1B. yo. K1.

ssk. yo. Rep from * twice more, then from * to ** once more. K3. yo. K1B. yo. K2. ssk. yo. K1B] twice. P2. K1B.

21st row: K1B. P2. K1B. [yo. K2tog. K3. yo. K1B. yo. K4. yo. ssk. K2tog. yo. Sl1. K2tog. psso. yo. K2tog. K2. yo. K1B. yo. K2. ssk. yo. *K1B. yo. K2tog. K2. yo. K1B. yo. K2. ssk. yo. Sl1. K2tog. psso. yo. ssk. K2tog. yo.** Sl1. K2tog. psso. yo. K2tog. K2. yo. K1B. yo. K2. ssk. yo. Rep from * twice more, then from * to ** once more. K4. yo. K1B. yo. K3. ssk. yo. K1B] twice. P2. K1B.

23rd row: K1B. P2. K1B. [(yo) twice. K2tog. K4. yo. K1B. yo. K3. ssk. yo. ssk. Sl1. K2tog. psso. yo. K2tog. K3. yo. K1B. yo. K3. ssk. yo. *K1B. yo. K2tog. K3. yo. K1B. yo. K3. ssk. yo.** (Sl1. K2tog. psso) twice. yo. K2tog. K3. yo. K1B. yo. K3. ssk. yo. Rep from * twice more, then from * to ** once more. Sl1. K2tog. psso. K2tog. yo. K2tog. K3. yo. K1B. yo. K4. ssk. (yo) twice. K1B] twice. P2. K1B.

24th row: Purl.

Panel VI

1st row: (RS). K1B. P2. [(K1B. yo) twice. *(K1B. yo) twice. ssk. K8. Sl1. K2tog. psso. (yo) twice. Sl1. K2tog. psso. K8. K2tog. yo. K1B.

yo.* Rep from * to * 4 times more. (K1B. yo) twice] twice. K1B. P2. K1B.

2nd row: Purl.

Rep 3rd to 12th rows as given for Panel IV, noting rep from * to * will be worked 5 times instead of 3 times. Rep 1st to 24th rows of Panel V, noting rep from * will be worked 5 times instead of 3 times. Rep 1st and 2nd rows of Panel VI, noting rep from * to * will be worked 5 times instead of 3 times.

Rep 3rd to 12th rows as given for Panel IV, noting rep from * to * will be worked 7 times instead of 3 times.

Rep 1st to 22nd rows of Panel V, noting rep from * will be worked 7 times instead of 3 times.

Panel VII

Work Panel VII as follows:

1st row: K1B. P2. K1B. [yo. K2tog. K4. yo. K1B. yo. K3. ssk. yo. ssk. Sl1. K2tog. psso. yo. K2tog. K3. yo. K1B. yo. K3. ssk. yo. *K1B. yo. K2tog. K3. yo. K1B. yo. K3. ssk. yo.** (Sl1. K2tog. psso) twice. yo. K2tog. K3. yo. K1B. yo. K3. ssk. yo. Rep from * twice more, then from * to ** once more. Sl1. K2tog. psso. K2tog. yo. K2tog. K3. yo. K1B. yo. K4. ssk. yo. K1B] twice. P2. K1B.

2nd row: Purl.

Panel VIII

Work Panel VIII as follows:

1st row: (RS). K1B. P2. K1B. [yo. *K1B. (yo. Sl1. K2tog. psso. K8. Sl1. K2tog. psso. yo) twice. Rep from * 8 times more. K1B. yo. K1B] twice. P2. K1B.

2nd and alt rows: Purl.

3rd row: K1B. P2. K1B. [yo. K1. *K1B. yo. K1. yo. ssk. K5. Sl1. K2tog. psso. yo. K2. yo. Sl1. K2tog. psso. K5. K2tog. yo. K1. yo. Rep from * 8 times more. K1B. K1. yo. K1B] twice. P2. K1B.

5th row: K1B. P2. K1B. [yo. K2tog. *K1B. (yo. ssk. K1) twice. K2. (K2tog. yo. ssk) twice. K2. (K1. K2tog. yo) twice. Rep from * 8 times more. K1B. ssk. yo. K1B] twice. P2. K1B.

7th row: K1B. P2. K1B. [yo. K2tog. yo. *K1B. (yo. ssk) 3 times. K1. (K2tog. yo. ssk) twice. K1. (K2tog. yo) 3 times. Rep from * 8 times more. K1B. yo. ssk. yo. K1B] twice. P2. K1B.

9th row: K1B. P2. K1B. [yo. K2tog. yo. *K3. yo. ssk. yo. K2. yo. Sl1. K2tog. psso. yo. ssk. K2tog. yo. Sl1. K2tog. psso. yo. K2. yo. K2tog. yo. Rep from * 8 times more. K3. yo. ssk. yo. K1B] twice. P2. K1B.

11th row: K1B. P2. K1B. [yo. K2tog. yo. *K5. (yo. ssk) twice. K1.
Sl1. K2tog. psso. (yo) twice. Sl1. K2tog. psso. K1. (K2tog. yo) twice.
Rep from * 8 times more. K5. yo. ssk. yo. K1B] twice. P2. K1B.

13th row: K1B. P2. K1B. {yo. K2tog. *yo. K7. yo. K2. [K2tog. (yo)
twice. ssk] twice. K2. Rep from * 8 times more. yo. K7. yo. ssk. yo.
K1B} twice. P2. K1B.

15th row: K1B. P2. K1B. [yo. K2tog. *yo. K9. yo. ssk. (yo. ssk.
K2tog. yo) twice. K2tog. Rep from * 8 times more. yo. K9. yo. ssk.
yo. K1B] twice. P2. K1B.

17th row: K1B. P2. K1B. [yo. K2tog. yo. K3. yo. ssk. *K1. K2tog. yo.
K3. yo. Sl1. K2tog. psso. (yo) twice. ssk. K2tog. (yo) twice. Sl1.
K2tog. psso. yo. K3. yo. ssk. Rep from * 8 times more. K1. K2tog.
yo. K3. yo. ssk. yo. K1B] twice. P2. K1B.

19th row: K1B. P2. K1B. [yo. K2tog. yo. K4. yo. ssk. *K1. K2tog. yo.
K4. (yo. ssk. K2tog. yo) twice. K4. yo. ssk. Rep from * 8 times more.
K1. K2tog. yo. K4. yo. ssk. yo. K1B] twice. P2. K1B.

21st row: K1B. P2. K1B. [yo. K2tog. yo. K5. (yo) twice. *(K5. yo)
twice. K1. ssk. K2tog. K1. yo. K5. yo. Rep from * 8 times more. K5.
(yo) twice. K5. yo. ssk. yo. K1B] twice. P2. K1B.

23rd row: K1B. P2. K1B. [yo. K2tog. yo. K1. yo. ssk. K1. K2tog. yo. K2. yo. *K5. yo. K1. (yo) twice. ssk. (K1. K2tog. yo) twice. (yo. ssk. K1) twice. K2tog. (yo) twice. K1. yo. Rep from * 8 times more. K5. yo. K2. yo. ssk. K1. K2tog. yo. K1. yo. ssk. yo. K1B] twice. P2. K1B.

25th row: K1B. P2. K1B. {yo. K2tog. K1. (yo) twice. ssk. yo. Sl1. K2tog. psso. yo. K2. yo. ssk. yo. *K5. yo. K2tog. yo. K2. yo. Sl1. K2tog. psso. yo.** [K2tog. (yo) twice. ssk] twice. yo. Sl1. K2tog. psso. yo. K2. yo. ssk. yo. Rep from * 8 times more, then from * to ** once. K2tog. (yo) twice. K1. ssk. yo. K1B} twice. P2. K1B.

27th row: K1B. P2. K1B. {yo. K2tog. [(yo) twice. ssk. K2tog] 3 times. yo. *K5. yo. K2tog. [K2tog. (yo) twice. ssk] 5 times. ssk. yo. Rep from * 8 times more. K5. (yo. ssk. K2tog. yo) 3 times. yo. ssk. yo. K1B} twice. P2. K1B.

29th row: K1B. P2. K1B. {yo. K2tog. yo. K1. [K2tog. (yo) twice. ssk] twice. K2tog. yo. ssk. yo. *K5. yo. K2tog. (yo. ssk K2tog. yo) 5 times. ssk. yo. Rep from * 8 times more. K5. yo. K2tog. (yo. ssk. K2tog. yo) twice. yo. ssk. K1. yo. Sl1 K1. psso. yo. K1B} twice. P2. K1B.

31st row: K1B. P2. K1B. [(yo. K2tog) twice. yo. (yo. ssk. K2tog. yo) twice. (yo. ssk) 3 times. *K1. (K2tog. yo) 3 times. (yo. ssk K2tog. yo) 4 times. (yo. ssk) 3 times. Rep from * 8 times more. K1. (K2tog. yo) 3 times. (yo. ssk. K2tog. yo) twice. yo. (ssk. yo) twice. K1B] twice. P2. K1B.

33rd row: K1B. P2. K1B. [yo. K2tog. K1. yo. (yo. ssk. K2tog. yo) 3 times. yo. K1. ssk. yo. *Sl1. K2tog. psso. yo. K2tog. K1. yo. (yo. ssk. K2tog. yo) 5 times. yo. K1. ssk. yo. Rep from * 8 times more. Sl1. K2tog. psso. yo. K2tog. K1. yo. (yo. ssk. K2tog. yo) 3 times. yo. K1. ssk. yo. K1B] twice. P2. K1B.

35th row: K1B. P2. K1B. [yo. K2tog. yo. (yo. ssk. K2tog. yo) 4 times. yo. Sl1. K2tog. psso. *yo. K2tog. yo. (yo. ssk. K2tog. yo) 6 times. yo. Sl1. K2tog. psso. Rep from * 8 times more. yo. ssk. yo. (yo. ssk. K2tog. yo) 4 times. yo. ssk. yo. K1B] twice. P2. K1B.

***36th row: Purl. Change to smaller circular needle and proceed as follows.

37th row: Knit to center st. (K1. yo. K1) all in center st. Knit to end of row.

38th and alt rows: Knit.

39th row: Knit to center st. (K1. yo. K1) all in center st. Knit to end of row.

41st row: As 39th row.

42nd row: Knit.

43rd row: (Picot row). Cast off 2 sts. * Slip rem st on right hand needle back onto left hand needle. Cast on 3 sts. Cast off 7 sts. Rep from * to last 2 sts. Slip rem st on right hand needle back onto left hand needle. Cast on 3 sts. Cast off 6 sts.***

Version II (Work from Charts and written instructions).

Notes: All wrong side rows are purled.

Work (yo) twice on WS rows as follows: P1. P1B. With pair of needles, cast on 9 sts. Proceed as follows, noting that work will be moved onto larger circular needle when pair of needles is no longer sufficient to accommodate sts.

1st row: (RS). K1B. P2. K1B. Work 1st row of Chart I, reading row from right to left. K1B. P2. K1B.

2nd and alt rows: Purl.

3rd row: K1B. P2. K1B. Work 3rd row of Chart I. K1B. P2. K1B. Chart I is now in position. Work Chart I to end of chart, ending with RS facing for next row.

Proceed as follows:

1st row: (RS). K1B. P2. K1B. yo. ssk. K2tog. (yo) twice. ssk. K2. K2tog. *(yo) twice. ssk. K2. [K2tog. (yo) twice. ssk] 3 times. K2. K2tog.* (yo) twice. ssk. K2. [K2tog. (yo) twice. ssk] 3 times. K2. Sl1.

K2tog. psso. (yo) twice. Sl1. K2tog. psso. K2. [K2tog. (yo) twice. ssk]
3 times. K2. K2tog. Rep from * to * once more. (yo) twice. ssk. K2.
K2tog. (yo) twice. ssk. K2tog. yo. K1B. P2. K1B.

2nd and alt rows: Purl.

3rd row: K1B. P2. K1B. Work 3rd row of Chart II. K1B. P2. K1B.

5th row: K1B. P2. K1B. Work 5th row of Cart II. K1B. P2. K1B.

Chart II is now in position.

Work Chart II to end of chart, ending with RS facing for next row.
Proceed as follows:

1st row: (RS). K1B. P2. K1B. Work 1st row of Chart III, reading row
from right to left. K1B. P2. K1B.

2nd and alt rows: Purl.

3rd row: K1B. P2. K1B. Work 3rd row of Chart III. K1B. P2. K1B.

Chart III is now in position.

Work Chart III to end of chart, ending with RS facing for next row.
Proceed as follows:

1st row: (RS). K1B. P2. K1B.

Work 1st row of Chart IV, reading row from right to left and noting
Sections A and A-1 will be worked 3 times. K1B. P2. K1B.

2nd and alt rows: Purl.

3rd row: K1B. P2. K1B. Work 3rd row of Chart IV, noting Sections A and A-1 will be worked 3 times. K1B. P2. K1B.

Chart IV is now in position.

Work Chart IV to end of chart, ending with RS facing for next row. Proceed as follows:

1st row: (RS). K1B. P2. K1B. (Work 1st row of Chart V, reading row from right to left and noting Section B will be worked 5 times) twice. P2. K1B.

2nd and alt rows: Purl.

3rd row: K1B. P2. K1B. (Work 3rd row of Chart V, noting Section B will be worked 5 times) twice. P2. K1B.

Chart V is now in position.

Work Chart V to end of chart, ending with RS facing for next row. Proceed as follows:

1st row: (RS). K1B. P2. K1B. (Work 1st row of Chart VI, reading row from right to left and noting Section C will be worked 5 times) twice. P2. K1B.

2nd row: Purl.

Proceed as follows:

1st row: (RS). K1B. P2. K1B. (Work

3rd row of Chart IV, reading row from right to left and noting Section A will be worked 5 times) twice. K1B. P2. K1B.

2nd and alt rows: Purl.

3rd row: K1B. P2. K1B. (Work 5th row of Chart IV, noting Section A will be worked 5 times) twice. K1B. P2. K1B.

Chart IV is now in position.

Work Chart IV to end of chart, ending with RS facing for next row. Proceed as follows:

1st row: (RS). K1B. P2. K1B. (Work 1st row of Chart V, reading row from right to left and noting Section B will be worked 5 times) twice. P2. K1B.

2nd and alt rows: Purl.

3rd row: K1B. P2. K1B. (Work 3rd row of Chart V, noting Section B will be worked 5 times) twice. P2. K1B.

Chart V is now in position.

Work Chart V to end of chart, ending with RS facing for next row. Proceed as follows:

1st row: (RS). K1B. P2. K1B. (Work 1st row of Chart VI, noting Section C will be worked 5 times) twice. P2. K1B.

2nd row: Purl.

Proceed as follows:

1st row: (RS). K1B. P2. K1B. (Work 3rd row of Chart IV, reading row from right to left and noting Section A will be worked 7 times) twice. K1B. P2. K1B.

2nd and alt rows: Purl.

3rd row: K1B. P2. K1B. (Work 4th row of Chart IV, noting Section A will be worked 7 times) twice. K1B. P2. K1B.

Chart IV is now in position.

Work Chart IV to end of chart, ending with RS facing for next row.

Proceed as follows:

1st row: (RS). K1B. P2. K1B (work 1st row of Chart V noting Section B will be worked 7 times) twice. P2. K1B.

2nd and alt rows: Purl.

Chart V is now in position.

Work Chart V until 21st row of Chart is complete.

Next row: Purl.

Proceed as follows:

1st row: (RS). K1B. P2. K1B. (Work 1st row of Chart VII, reading row from right to left and noting Section D will be worked 7 times) twice. P2. K1B.

Next row: Purl.

Proceed as follows:

1st row: (RS). K1B. P2. K1B. (Work 1st row of Chart VIII, reading row from right to left) twice. P2. K1B.

2nd and alt rows: Purl.

3rd row: K1B. P2. K1B.

(Work 2nd row of Chart VIII) twice. P2. K1B. Chart VIII is now in position.

Work Chart VIII to end of chart, ending with RS facing for next row.

Rep from *** to *** as given for Version I.

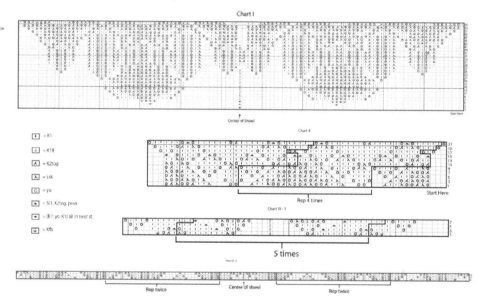

Knit Shawl

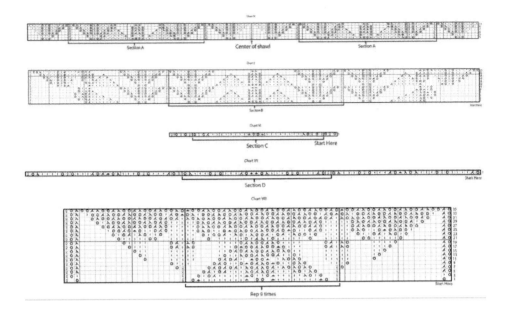

II. Pastoral Lace Knit Shawl

MATERIALS

Patons® Grace™ (1.75 oz/50 g; 136 yds/125 m)

Ginger (62027) 5 balls

Size U.S. 6 (4 mm) circular knitting needle 36" [91.5 cm] long or size needed to obtain gauge.

Stitch marker.

ABBREVIATIONS

Alt = Alternate(ing)

Approx = Approximate(ly)

Inc = Increas(e)(es)(ing)

K = Knit

K2tog = Knit next 2 stitches together

M1 = Make 1 stitch by picking up horizontal loop lying before next stitch and knitting into back of loop

P = Purl

P2sso = Pass 2 slipped stitches over

Pat = Pattern

Rep = Repeat

RS = Right side

Sl2K = Slip next 2 stitches knitwise

SM = Slip marker

Ssk = Slip next 2 stitches knitwise one at a time. Pass them back onto left-hand needle, then knit through back loops together.

St(s) = Stitch(es)

WS = Wrong side

Yo = Yarn over

MEASUREMENTS

Approx 45" [114.5 cm] wide x 26" [66 cm] deep.

GAUGE

22 sts and 30 rows = 4" [10 cm] in stocking st.

INSTRUCTIONS

Cast on 7 sts.

1st row: (RS). K3. yo. K1. yo. K3. 9 sts. 2nd row: K3. Purl to last 3 sts. K3.

3rd row: K3. yo. K1. yo. Place marker before next st. K1. yo. K1. yo. K3. 13 sts.

4th row: As 2nd row.

5th row: K3. yo. Knit to marker. yo. K1. yo. Knit to last 3 sts. yo. K3.

6th row: As 2nd row. Rep 5th and 6th rows, inc 4 sts on next and every following alt row until there are 125 sts, ending on a WS row. Note: Move marker every row, noting marker is placed on needle before center st.

Proceed in Lace Pat (see chart):

1st row: K3. yo. K2tog. K2. yo. *K1. yo. K2. ssk. P1. K2tog. K2. yo.*
Rep from * to * until 5 sts before marker. K1. yo. K2. ssk. yo. SM.
K1. yo. K2tog. K2. yo. Rep from * to * until last 8 sts. K1. yo. K2.
ssk. yo. K3. 129 sts.

2nd and alt rows: K3. Knit all knit sts and purl all purl and yo as they
appear to last 3 sts. K3.

3rd row: K3. yo. P1. K2tog. K1. yo. K3. *yo. K1. ssk. P1. K2tog. K1.
yo. K3.* Rep from * to * until 4 sts before marker. yo. K1. ssk. P1.
yo. SM. K1. yo. P1. K2tog. K1. yo. K3. Rep from * to * until last 7
sts. yo. K1. ssk. P1. yo. K3. 133 sts.

5th row: K3. yo. K1. *P1. K2tog. yo. K5. yo. ssk.* Rep from * to *
until 2 sts before marker. P1. K1. yo. SM. K1. yo. K1. Rep from * to
* until last 5 sts. P1. K1. yo. K3. 137 sts.

7th row: K3. *yo. K2. P1. K2. yo. ssk. K1. K2tog.* Rep from * to *
until 5 sts before marker. yo. K2. P1. K2. yo. SM. K1. Rep from * to
* until last 8 sts. yo. K2. P1. K2. yo. K3. 141 sts.

9th row: K3. *yo. K3. P1. K3. yo. Sl2K. K1. p2sso.* Rep from * to *
until 7 sts before marker. yo. K3. P1. K3. yo. SM. K1. Rep from * to
* until last 10 sts. yo. K3. P1. K3. yo. K3. 145 sts.

10th row: As 2nd row. Rep 1st to 10th rows 9 times more. 325 sts.

Proceed in Border Pat as follows:

1st and 2nd rows: As 1st and 2nd rows of Lace Pat. 329 sts.

3rd row: K3. yo. K1. *K2tog. K1. yo. K3. yo. K1. ssk. P1.* Rep from * to * until 10 sts before marker. K2tog. K1. yo. K3. yo. K1. ssk. K1. yo. SM. K1. yo. K1. Rep from * to * until last 13 sts. K2tog. K1. yo. K3. yo. K1. ssk. K1. yo. K3. 333 sts.

4th row: As 2nd row.

5th row: K3. yo. K2. *K2tog. yo. K5. yo. ssk. P1.* Rep from * to * until 11 sts before marker. K2tog. yo. K5. yo. ssk. K2. yo. SM. K1. yo. K2. Rep from * to * until last 14 sts. K2tog. yo. K5. yo. ssk. K2. yo. K3. 337 sts.

6th and alt rows: K3. Purl to last 3 sts. K3. 7th row: K3. yo. K2. ssk. *yo. K7. yo. Sl2K. K1. p2sso.* Rep from * to * until 13 sts before marker. yo. K7. yo. K2. K2tog. K2. yo. SM. K1. yo. K2. ssk. Rep from * to * until last 14 sts. yo. K7. yo. K2tog. K2. yo. K3. 341 sts.

9th row: K3. yo. K3. ssk. *yo. K3. M1. K1. M1. K3. yo. Sl2K. K1. p2sso.* Rep from * to * until 13 sts before marker. yo. K3. M1. K1. M1. K3. yo. K1. K2tog. K3. yo. SM. K1. yo. K3. ssk. Rep from * to * until last 15 sts. yo. K3. M1. K1. M1. K3. yo. K2tog. K3. yo. K3. 415 sts.

11th row: K3. yo. K4. ssk. *yo. K4. M1. K1. M1. K4. yo. Sl2K. K1. p2s-so.* Rep from * to * until 15 sts before marker. yo. K4. M1. K1. M1. K4. yo. K2tog. K4. yo. SM. K1. yo. K4. ssk. Rep from * to * until last 18 sts. yo. K4. M1. K1. M1. K4. yo. K2tog. K4. yo. K3. 483 sts.

Cast off loosely knitwise (WS).

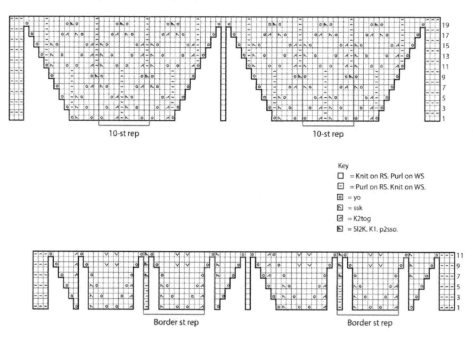

Key
☐ = Knit on RS. Purl on WS.
⊟ = Purl on RS. Knit on WS.
⊡ = yo
☒ = ssk
☒ = K2tog
☒ = Sl2K. K1. p2sso.

III. Ashbridge's Bay Knit Shawl

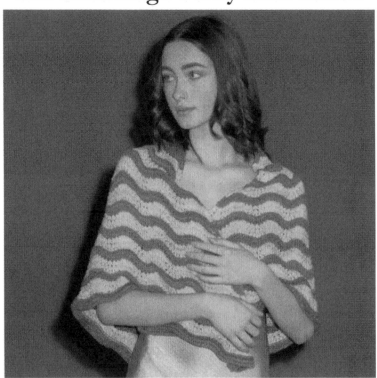

MATERIALS

Patons® Kroy FX™ (1.75 oz/50 g; 166 yds/152 m) Contrast A

Mossy Colors (57705) 3 balls Contrast B

Seashell Colors (57703) 3 balls

Size U.S. 5 (3.75 mm) circular knitting needle 29" [73.5 cm] long or size needed to obtain gauge.

Stitch marker.

Yarn needle.

ABBREVIATIONS

Alt = Alternat(e)(ing)

Approx = Approximately

K = Knit

K2tog = Knit next 2 stitches together

P = Purl

Pat = Pattern

PM = Place marker

Rep = Repeat

RS = Right side

SM = Slip marker

St(s) = Stitch(es)

WS = Wrong side

Yo = Yarn over

MEASUREMENTS

Approx 30" deep x 60" wide [76 x 152.5 cm].

GAUGE

24 sts and 44 rows = 4" [10 cm] in garter st.

Knit Shawl

INSTRUCTIONS

Notes:

• Shawl is worked from center back neck edge down.

• A small Tab piece is knit first with sts picked up around around sides of Tab to create a base for remainder of Shawl.

• Move marker beside center st up every row as work progresses.

Tab:

With A, cast on 3 sts. Knit 5 rows.

Next row: Knit to end of row.

Turn work 90 degrees.

Pick up and knit 3 sts along garter tab edge (1 st picked up per garter ridge).

Pick up and knit 3 sts across tab cast on edge. 9 sts.

1st row: (RS) K3. yo. K1. yo. PM. K1. yo. K1. yo. K3. 13 sts.

2nd row: Knit.

3rd row: K3. yo. Knit to marker. yo. SM. K1. yo. Knit to last 3 sts. yo. K3. 17 sts.

4th row: Knit. Rep 3rd and 4th rows until you have 117 sts, ending on a WS row.

Break A. Join B.

Proceed in Old Shale Pat as follows (see Chart):

1st row: (RS). With B, K3. yo. *(K2tog) 3 times. (K1. yo) 6 times. (K2tog) 3 times. Rep from * to 1 st before marker. K1. yo. SM. K1. yo. K1. **(K2tog) 3 times. (yo. K1) 6 times. (K2tog) 3 times. Rep from ** to last 3 sts. yo. K3. 121 sts.

2nd and alt rows (unless otherwise indicated): K3. Purl to last 3 sts. K3.

3rd row: K3. yo. Knit to 1 st before marker. yo. SM. K1. yo. Knit to last 3 sts. yo. K3. 125 sts.

5th row: K3. yo. K2. *(K2tog) 3 times. (K1. yo) 6 times. (K2tog) 3 times. Rep from * to 3 sts before marker. K3. yo. SM. K1. yo. K3. **(K2tog) 3 times. (yo. K1) 6 times. (K2tog) 3 times. Rep from ** to last 5 sts. K2. yo. K3. 129 sts.

7th row: As 3rd row. 133 sts.

9th row: K3. yo. K4. *(K2tog) 3 times. (K1. yo) 6 times. (K2tog) 3 times. Rep from * to 5 sts before marker. K5. yo. SM. K1. yo. K5. **(K2tog) 3 times. (yo. K1) 6 times. (K2tog) 3 times. Rep from ** to last 7 sts. K4. yo. K3. 137 sts. 10th row: As 2nd row. Break B. Join A. 11th row: With A, as 3rd row. 141 sts

12th row: Knit.

13th to 16th rows: Rep 11th and 12th rows twice more. 149 sts.

17th row: As 11th row. 153 sts.

18th and alt rows: As 2nd row. Break A. Join B.

19th row: With B, K3. yo. (K1. yo) 3 times. (K2tog) 6 times. *(K1. yo) 6 times. (K2tog) 6 times. Rep from * to 4 sts before marker. (K1. yo) 4 times. SM. K1. (yo. K1) 4 times. (K2tog) 6 times. **(yo. K1) 6 times. (K2tog) 6 times. Rep from * to last 6 sts. (yo. K1) 4 times. K2. 157 sts.

21st row: As 3rd row. 161 sts. 23rd row: K3. yo. K3. (yo. K1) twice. yo. (K2tog) 6 times. *(K1. yo) 6 times. (K2tog) 6 times. Rep from * to 6 sts before marker. (K1. yo) 3 times. K3. yo. SM. K1. yo. K3. (yo. K1) 3 times. (K2tog) 6 times **(yo. K1) 6 times. (K2tog) 6 times. Rep from ** to last 8 sts. (yo. K1) 3 times. K2. yo. K3. 165 sts.

25th row: As 3rd row. 169 sts.

27th row: K3. yo. K5. (yo. K1) twice. yo. (K2tog) 6 times. *(K1. yo) 6 times. (K2tog) 6 times. Rep from * to 8 sts before marker. (K1. yo) 3 times. K5. yo. SM. K1. yo. K5. (yo. K1) 3 times. (K2tog) 6 times. **(yo. K1) 6 times. (K2tog) 6 times. Rep from ** to last 10 sts. (yo. K1) 3 times. K4. yo. K3. 173 sts. Break B. Join A.

29th to 36th rows: Work as 11th to 18th rows. 189 sts. These 36 rows form Old Shale Pat.

Rep Old Shale Pat 3 times more. 405 sts.

Cast off loosely knitwise with B.

IV. Sparkling Lace Knit Shawl

MATERIALS

Red Heart® Roll With It Sparkle™ (5.29 oz/150 g; 561 yds/513 m)

Amethyst (7001) 2 balls

Size U.S. 6 (4mm) circular knitting needle 29" [73.5 cm] long or size needed to obtain gauge.

3 stitch markers.

Tapestry needle.

ABBREVIATIONS

Alt = Alternate(ing)

Approx = Approximately

K = Knit

K1tbl = Knit next stitch through back loop

K2tog = Knit next 2 stitches together

P2sso = Pass 2 slipped stitches over

PM = Place marker

Rep = Repeat

RS = Right side

Sl2K = Slip next 2 stitches together knitwise

SM = Slip marker

Ssk = Slip next 2 stitches one at a time. Pass them back onto left-hand needle, then knit through the back loops together.

St(s) = Stitch(es)

WS = Wrong side

Knit Shawl

Yo = Yarn over

MEASUREMENTS

Approx 54" [137 cm] wide x 25" [63.5 cm] deep.

GAUGE

22 sts and 30 rows = 4" [10 cm] in stocking st.

INSTRUCTIONS

Garter Tab Cast On

Cast on 3 sts. Do not join. Working back and forth across needle in rows, proceed as follows: Knit 6 rows (garter st).

Next row: K3. Pick up and knit 3 sts along length of 6 rows just worked. Pick up and knit 3 sts along cast on edge of work. 9 sts.

Body

1st row: (RS). K3. (yo. K1) 3 times. yo. K3. 13 sts. 2nd row: K3. Purl to last 3 sts. K3.

3rd row: K3. yo. K3. yo. PM. K1. yo. K3. yo. K3. 17 sts 4th row: As 2nd row.

5th row: K3. yo. Knit to marker. yo. SM. K1. yo. Knit to last 3 sts. yo. K3. 21 sts.

6th row: K3. Purl to last 3 sts. K3. Rep last 2 rows until there are 261 sts, ending on a WS row.

Lace Border (See chart).

1st row: K3. yo. K1. *K2tog. yo. K1tbl. K1. K2tog. yo. K1tbl. yo. ssk. K1. K1tbl. yo. ssk. K1.* Rep from * to * to marker. yo. SM. K1. yo. K1. Rep from * to * to last 3 sts. yo. K3. 265 sts.

2nd and alt rows: K3. Purl to last 3 sts. K3.

3rd row: K3. yo. K2. *(K2tog. yo. K1) twice. K1tbl. (K1. yo. ssk) twice. K1.* Rep from * to * to 1 st before marker. K1. yo. SM. K1. yo. K2.* Rep from * to * to last 4 sts. K1. yo. K3. 269 sts.

5th row: K3. yo. K2. K2tog. *yo. K1tbl. K2tog. yo. K1tbl. K3. K1tbl. yo. ssk. K1tbl. yo. Sl2k. K1. P2sso.* Rep from * to * 15 sts before marker. yo. K1tbl. K2tog. yo. K1tbl. K3. K1tbl. yo. ssk. K1tbl. yo. ssk. K2. yo. SM. K1. yo. K2. K2tog. Rep from * to * to last 18 sts. yo. K1tbl. K2tog. yo. K1tbl. K3. K1tbl. yo. ssk. K1tbl. yo. ssk. K2. yo. K3. 273 sts.

7th row: K3. yo. K2. K1tbl. K1. *(K1tbl. K2tog. yo) twice. (K1tbl. yo. ssk) twice. K1tbl. K1.* Rep from * to * 3 sts before marker. K1tbl. K2. yo. SM. K1. yo. K2. K1tbl. K1. Rep from * to * to last 6 sts. K1tbl. K2. yo. K3. 277 sts.

9th row: K3. yo. K1. K1tbl. yo. ssk. K1. *(K2tog. yo. K1tbl) twice. K1. (K1tbl. yo. ssk) twice. K1.* Rep from * to * 4 sts before marker.

K2tog. yo. K1tbl. K1. yo. SM. K1. yo. K1. K1tbl. yo. ssk. K1. Rep from * to * to last 7 sts. K2tog. yo. K1tbl. K1. yo. K3. 281 sts.

11th row: K3. yo. K3. K1tbl. yo. K2tog. *yo. K1tbl. K2. yo. ssk. K1. K2tog. yo. K2. K1tbl. yo. Sl2K. K1. P2sso.* Rep from * to * to 4 sts before marker. yo. K1tbl. K3. yo. SM. K1. yo. K3. K1tbl. yo. K2tog. Rep from * to * to last 7 sts. yo. K1tbl. K3. yo. K3. 285 sts.

13th row: K3. yo. K2tog. yo. K1. K2tog. yo. K1tbl. K1. *K1tbl. yo. ssk. K1.yo. ssk. K1. K2tog. yo. K1. K2tog. yo. K1tbl. K1.* Rep from * to * to 6 sts before marker. K1tbl. yo. ssk. K1. yo. ssk. yo. SM. K1. yo. K2tog. yo. K1. K2tog. yo. K1tbl. K1. Rep from * to * to last 9 sts. K1tbl. yo. ssk. K1. yo. ssk. yo. K3. 289 sts.

15th row: K3. yo. K2tog. yo. K1tbl. K2. yo. ssk. K1. *K2tog. yo. K2. K1tbl. yo. Sl2K. K1. P2sso. yo. K1tbl. K2. yo. ssk. K1.* Rep from * to * to 7 sts before marker. K2tog. yo. K2. K1tbl. yo. ssk. yo. SM. K1. yo. K2tog. yo. K1tbl. K2. yo. ssk. K1. Rep from * to * to last 10 sts. K2tog. yo. K2. K1tbl. yo. ssk. yo. K3. 293 sts.

17th row: K3. yo. K1. K1tbl. (K1. yo. ssk) twice. K1. *(K2tog. yo. K1) twice. K1tbl. (K1. yo. ssk) twice. K1.* Rep from * to * to 8 sts before marker. (K2tog. yo. K1) twice. K1tbl. K1. yo. SM. K1. yo. K1.

K1tbl. (K1. yo. ssk) twice. K1. Rep from * to * to last 17 sts. (K2tog. yo. K1) twice. K1tbl. K1. yo. K3. 297 sts.

19th row: K3. yo. K4. K1tbl. yo. ssk. K1tbl. yo. Sl2K. K1. P2sso. *yo. K1tbl. K2tog. yo. K1tbl. K3. K1tbl. yo. ssk. K1tbl. yo. Sl2k. K1. P2sso.* Rep from * to * to 8 sts before marker. yo. K1tbl. K2tog. yo. K1tbl. K4. yo. SM. K1. yo. K4. K1tbl. yo. ssk. K1tbl. yo. Sl2K. K1. P2sso. Rep from * to * to last 11 sts. yo. K1tbl. K2tog. yo. K1tbl. K4. yo. K3. 301 sts.

21st row: K3. yo. K1tbl. K2tog. yo. K1tbl. yo. ssk. K1tbl. yo. ssk. K1tbl. K1. *(K1tbl. K2tog. yo) twice. K1tbl. (yo. ssk. K1tbl) twice. K1.* Rep from * to * to 10 sts before marker. (K1tbl. K2tog. yo) twice. K1tbl. yo. ssk. K1tbl. yo. SM. K1. yo. K1tbl. K2tog. yo. K1tbl. (yo. ssk. K1tbl) twice. K1. Rep from * to * to last 13 sts. (K1tbl. K2tog. yo) twice. K1tbl. yo. ssk. K1tbl. yo. K3.

23rd row: K3. yo. K1tbl. K2tog. yo. K1tbl. K1. (K1tbl. yo. ssk) twice. K1. *(K2tog. yo. K1tbl) twice. K1. (K1tbl. yo. ssk) twice. K1.* Rep from * to * to 11 sts before marker. (K2tog. yo. K1tbl) twice. K1. K1tbl. yo. ssk. K1. yo. SM. K1. yo. K1tbl. K2tog. yo. K1tbl. K1. (K1tbl. yo. ssk) twice. K1. Rep from * to * to last 14 sts. (K2tog. yo. K1tbl) twice. K1. K1tbl. yo. ssk. K1. yo. K3. 305 sts.

25th row: K3. *yo. K1tbl. K2. yo. ssk. K1. K2tog. yo. K2. K1tbl. yo. Sl2K. K1. P2sso.* Rep from * to * to marker, ending nal rep with ssk. yo. SM. K1. Rep from * to * to last 3 sts, ending nal rep with ssk. yo. K3. 309 sts.

27th row: K3. yo. *K1tbl. yo. ssk. K1. yo. ssk. K1. K2tog. yo. K1. K2tog. yo. K1tbl. K1.* Rep from * to * to marker, omitting last K1 from nal rep. yo. SM. K1. yo. Rep from * to * to last 3 sts, omitting last K1 from nal rep. yo. K3. 313 sts.

29th row: K3. yo. K1. *K2tog. yo. K2. K1tbl. yo. Sl2K. K1. P2sso. yo. K1tbl. K2. yo. ssk. K1.* Rep from * to * marker. yo. SM. K1. yo. K1. Rep from * to * to last 3 sts. yo. K3. 317 sts.

30th row: K3. Purl to last 3 sts. K3. Rep 1st to 30th rows once more. 377 sts.

Final Border

1st row: K3. yo. K8. yo. K1tbl. yo. *K13. yo. K1tbl. yo.* Rep from * to * to 8 sts before marker. K8. yo. SM. K1. yo. K8. yo. K1tbl. yo. Rep from * to * to last 11 sts. K8. yo. K3,

2nd and alt rows: K3. Purl to last 3 sts. K3.

3rd row: K3. yo. K10. yo. K1tbl. yo. *K15. Yo. K1tbl. yo.* Rep from * to * to 10 sts before marker. K10. yo. SM. K1. yo. K10. yo. K1tbl.

yo. Rep from * to * to last 13 sts. K10. yo. K3. 5th row: K3. yo. K12. yo. K1tbl. yo. *K17. yo. K1tbl. yo.* Rep from * to * to 12 sts before marker K12. yo. SM. K1. yo. K12. yo. K1tbl. yo. Rep from * to * to last 15 sts. K12. yo. K3. Knit 3 rows (garter st).

Cast off loosely.

V. Sharp Wedges Knit Shawl

MATERIALS

Red Heart® Super Saver® Brushed™ (5 oz/141 g; 253 yds/231 m)

Contrast A

Dusty Pink (5071) 1 ball Contrast B

Soft Mink (5030) 1 ball

Size U.S. 10 (6 mm) Susan Bates® Silvalume® circular knitting needle 36" [91.5 cm] long or size needed to obtain gauge.

Susan Bates® split ring stitch marker.

ABBREVIATIONS

Approx = Approximately

K = Knit

Kfb = Increase 1 stitch by knitting into front and back of next stitch

PM = Place marker

Rem = Remaining

Rep = Repeat

RS = Right side

St(s) = Stitch(es)

Sl1P = Slip next stitch purlwise

WS = Wrong side

MEASUREMENTS

Approx 20" [51 cm] deep x 65" [165 cm] wide.

GAUGE

15 sts and 28 rows = 4" [10 cm] in garter st .

INSTRUCTIONS

With A, cast on 3 sts. Work back and forth across needle in rows as follows:

1st row: (WS). Kfb. K1. Kfb. 5 sts.

2nd row: Kfb. Knit to last st. Kfb.

Rep last row until there are 13 sts.

Do not break A. Join B.

Next row: (RS). With B, as 2nd row. 15 sts.

Next row: Kfb. Knit to last 3 sts.

Turn.

Leave rem sts unworked.

Next row: Sl1P. PM on last st worked (Sl1P). Knit to last st. Kfb.

Next row: Kfb. Knit to 2 sts before marked st.

Turn.

Leave rem sts on a spare needle. Rep last 2 rows 8 times more

Next row: Sl1P. Knit to last st. Kfb.

Next row: Kfb. Knit across all sts to last st. Kfb. 37 sts. Break B.

Next row: With A, Kfb. Knit to last 5 sts.

Turn.

Leave rem sts on a spare needle.

Next row: Sl1P. PM on last st worked (Sl1P). Knit to last st. Kfb.

Next row: Kfb. Knit to 4 sts before marked st. Turn. Leave rem sts on a spare needle. Rep last 2 rows 8 times more.

Next row: Sl1P. Knit to last st. Kfb. Do not break A. Join B. 57 sts.

Next row: (RS). With B, Kfb. Knit across all sts to last st. Kfb. 59 sts.

Next row: Kfb. Knit to last 7 sts. Turn. Leave rem sts on a spare needle.

Next row: Sl1P. PM on last st worked (Sl1P). Knit to last st. Kfb.

Next row: Kfb. Knit to 6 sts before marked st.

Turn.

Leave rem sts on a spare needle. Rep last 2 rows 8 times more

Next row: Sl1P. Knit to last st. Kfb.

Next row: (RS). Kfb. Knit across all sts to last st. Kfb. 81 sts. Break B.

Next row: With A, Kfb. Knit to last 5 sts.

Turn.

Leave rem sts on a spare needle.

Next row: Sl1P. PM on last st worked (Sl1P). Knit to last st. Kfb.

Next row: Kfb. Knit to 4 sts before marked st.

Turn.

Leave rem sts on a spare needle. Rep last 2 rows 10 times more.

Next row: Sl1P. Knit to last st. Kfb. 105 sts. Do not break A. Join B.

Next row: (RS). With B, Kfb. Knit across all sts to last st. Kfb. 107 sts.

Next row: Kfb. Knit to last 7 sts.

Turn.

Leave rem sts on a spare needle.

Next row: Sl1P. PM on last st worked (Sl1P). Knit to last st. Kfb.

Next row: Kfb. Knit to 6 sts before marked st. Turn. Leave rem sts on a spare needle. Rep last 2 rows 10 times more

Next row: Sl1P. Knit to last st. Kfb.

Next row: Kfb. Knit across all sts to last st. Kfb. 133 sts. Break B.

Next row: With A, Kfb. Knit to last 10 sts. Turn. Leave rem sts on a spare needle.

Next row: Sl1P. PM on last st worked (Sl1P). Knit to last st. Kfb.

Next row: Kfb. Knit to 9 sts before marked st. Turn. Leave rem sts on a spare needle. Rep last 2 rows 10 times more.

Next row: Sl1P. Knit to last st. Kfb. 157 sts. Break A. Join B.

Next row: (RS). With B, Kfb. Knit across all sts to last st. Kfb. 159 sts.

Next row: Kfb. Knit to last 12 sts. Turn. Leave rem sts on a spare needle.

Next row: Sl1P. PM on last st worked (Sl1P). Knit to last st. Kfb.

Next row: Kfb. Knit to 11 sts before marked st.

Turn.

Leave rem sts on a spare needle. Rep last 2 rows 10 times more.

Next row: Sl1P. Knit to last st. Kfb.

Next row: Kfb. Knit across all sts to last st. Kfb. 185 sts.

Next row: With A, Kfb. Knit to last 15 sts.

Turn.

Leave rem sts on a spare needle.

Next row: Sl1P. PM on last st worked (Sl1P). Knit to last st. Kfb.

Next row: Kfb. Knit to 14 sts before marked st.

Turn.

Leave rem sts on a spare needle. Rep last 2 rows 10 times more.

Next row: Sl1P. Knit to last st. Kfb. Break A. Join B.

Next row: (RS). With B, Kfb. Knit across all sts to last st. Kfb. 211 sts.

Next row: Kfb. Knit to last 17 sts.

Turn.

Leave rem sts on a spare needle.

Next row: Sl1P. PM on last st worked (Sl1P). Knit to last st. Kfb.

Next row: Kfb. Knit to 16 sts before marked st.

Turn.

Leave rem sts on a spare needle. Rep last 2 rows 10 times more

Next row: Sl1P. Knit to last st. Kfb.

Next row: Kfb. Knit across all sts to last st. Kfb. 237 sts.

Cast off loosely

VI. Airy Lace Knit Shawl

MATERIALS

Patons® Linen™ (3.5 oz/100 g; 275 yds/251 m) Peony (14010) 3
balls

Size U.S. 6 (4 mm)

Susan Bates® Silvalume® circular knitting needle 36" [91.5 cm] long
or size needed to obtain gauge.

Susan Bates® stitch marker.

ABBREVIATIONS

Alt = Alternate(ing)

Approx = Approximate(ly)

Beg = Beginning

Inc = Increas(e)(es)(ing)

K = Knit

K2tog = Knit next 2 stitches together

M1 = Make 1 stitch by picking up horizontal loop lying before next stitch and knitting into back of loop

P = Purl

P2sso = Pass 2 slipped stitches over

Pat = Pattern

Rep = Repeat

RS = Right side

Sl2K = Slip next 2 stitches knitwise

SM = Slip marker

Ssk = Slip next 2 stitches knitwise one at a time. Pass them back onto left-hand needle, then knit through back loops together.

St(s) = Stitch(es)

WS = Wrong side

Yo = Yarn over

MEASUREMENTS

Approx 72" [183 cm] wide x 34" [86.5 cm] deep.

GAUGE

24 sts and 32 rows = 4" [10 cm] in stocking st.

INSTRUCTIONS

Beg at center back neck, cast on 7 sts.

1st row: (RS). K3. yo. K1. yo. K3. 9 sts.

2nd row: K3. Purl to last 3 sts. K3.

3rd row: K3. yo. K1. yo. Place marker before next st. K1. yo. K1. yo. K3. 13 sts.

4th row: As 2nd row.

5th row: K3. yo. Knit to marker. yo. K1. yo. Knit to last 3 sts. yo. K3.

6th row: As 2nd row. Rep 5th and 6th rows, inc 4 sts on next and every following alt row until there are 125 sts, ending on a WS row.

Note: Move marker every row, noting marker is placed on needle before center st.

Proceed in Lace Pat (see chart):

1st row: K3. yo. K2tog. K2. yo. *K1. yo. K2. ssk. P1. K2tog. K2. yo.* Rep from * to * until 5 sts before marker. K1. yo. K2. ssk. yo. SM. K1. yo. K2tog. K2. yo. Rep from * to * until last 8 sts. K1. yo. K2. ssk. yo. K3. 129 sts.

2nd and alt rows: K3. Knit all knit sts and purl all purl and yo as they appear to last 3 sts. K3.

3rd row: K3. yo. P1. K2tog. K1. yo. K3. *yo. K1. ssk. P1. K2tog. K1. yo. K3.* Rep from * to * until 4 sts before marker. yo. K1. ssk. P1. yo. SM. K1. yo. P1. K2tog. K1. yo. K3. Rep from * to * until last 7 sts. yo. K1. ssk. P1. yo. K3. 133 sts.

5th row: K3. yo. K1. *P1. K2tog. yo. K5. yo. ssk.* Rep from * to * until 2 sts before marker. P1. K1. yo. SM. K1. yo. K1. Rep from * to * until last 5 sts. P1. K1. yo. K3. 137 sts.

7th row: K3. *yo. K2. P1. K2. yo. ssk. K1. K2tog.* Rep from * to * until 5 sts before marker. yo. K2. P1. K2. yo. SM. K1. Rep from * to * until last 8 sts. yo. K2. P1. K2. yo. K3. 141 sts.

9th row: K3. *yo. K3. P1. K3. yo. Sl2K. K1. p2sso.* Rep from * to * until 7 sts before marker. yo. K3. P1. K3. yo. SM. K1. Rep from * to * until last 10 sts. yo. K3. P1. K3. yo. K3. 145 sts.

10th row: As 2nd row.

Rep 1st to 10th rows 9 times more. 325 sts.

Proceed in Border Pat as follows:

1st and 2nd rows: As 1st and 2nd rows of Lace Pat. 329 sts.

3rd row: K3. yo. K1. *K2tog. K1. yo. K3. yo. K1. ssk. P1.* Rep from * to * until 10 sts before marker. K2tog. K1. yo. K3. yo. K1. ssk. K1. yo. SM. K1. yo. K1. Rep from * to * until last 13 sts. K2tog. K1. yo. K3. yo. K1. ssk. K1. yo. K3. 333 sts.

4th row: As 2nd row. 5th row: K3. yo. K2. *K2tog. yo. K5. yo. ssk. P1.* Rep from * to * until 11 sts before marker. K2tog. yo. K5. yo. ssk. K2. yo. SM. K1. yo. K2. Rep from * to * until last 14 sts. K2tog. yo. K5. yo. ssk. K2. yo. K3. 337 sts.

6th and alt rows: K3. Purl to last 3 sts. K3. 7th row: K3. yo. K2. ssk. *yo. K7. yo. Sl2K. K1. p2sso.* Rep from * to * until 13 sts before marker. yo. K7. yo. K2. K2tog. K2. yo. SM. K1. yo. K2. ssk. Rep from * to * until last 14 sts. yo. K7. yo. K2tog. K2. yo. K3. 341 sts.

9th row: K3. yo. K3. ssk. *yo. K3. M1. K1. M1. K3. yo. Sl2K. K1. p2sso.* Rep from * to * until 13 sts before marker. yo. K3. M1. K1. M1. K3. yo. K1. K2tog. K3. yo. SM. K1. yo. K3. ssk. Rep from * to * until last 15 sts. yo. K3. M1. K1. M1. K3. yo. K2tog. K3. yo. K3. 415 sts.

11th row: K3. yo. K4. ssk. *yo. K4. M1. K1. M1. K4. yo. Sl2K. K1.*
Rep from * to * until 15 sts before marker. yo. K4. M1. K1. M1. K4.
yo. K2tog. K4. yo. SM. K1. yo. K4. ssk. Rep from * to * until last 18
sts. yo. K4. M1. K1. M1. K4. yo. K2tog. K4. yo. K3. 483 sts.
Cast off loosely knitwise (WS).

Made in United States
Orlando, FL
06 December 2024

55071412R00035